W0006096

GOD
LIVES IN INDIA

R. K. KARANJIA

SAI
TOWERS

PUBLISHING

© Sai Towers

Reprint 1999

ISBN: 81-86822-27-5

Published by:
Sai Towers Publishing
Sai Towers Brindavan
23/1142 Vijayalakshmi Colony
Kadugudi, Bangalore 560 067
Ph   : (080) 8451648
Fax   : (080) 8451649
E-mail : saitower@vsnl.com
Web   : saitowers.com

Printed at
D.K. Fine Art Press Pvt. Ltd.
Delhi 110 052 INDIA

GW01087090

CONTENTS

INTRODUCTION

Puttaparthi, the obscure tiny village set in a narrow farming valley in India's southern state of Andhra Pradesh, is fast emerging as the world's largest pilgrimage centre. Millions of seekers of truth from all corners of the globe pour into this small stone and thatched village nestling in the brown - capped hills to pay obeisance to the incredible Sathya Sai Baba.

Judging by His ever increasing following, Sai Baba has apparently been accepted by millions as a cosmic phenomenon. Never before in the recorded history of mankind has any Divine Personage been adored and revered by the multitudes during the course of His lifetime as Sai Baba is today. His proliferating tribe of devotees, estimated at over 80 million, is spread over 130 countries of the world, and periodically assemble in over 5,000 Sai Centres to reaffirm their faith in His divinity and seek light on the path to Self-realization.

On May 23, 1940, thirteen year old Sathya Narayana Raju made the historic announcement: "I am Sai Baba. My mission in this earthly sojourn shall be to lead man along the path of Dharma (righteousness) back to My feet. I have come to re-establish the Vedic way of life, to reinstate the supremacy of the spirit over matter, and to lead man back to the life of the spirit."

For practically six decades now, Sai Baba has been unequivocally demonstrating His supernatural powers, giving visions of His Divinity and unambiguously reiterating that He is God incarnate come to re-establish righteousness in the world. "I have come in order to repair the ancient highway leading man to God," He adds.

But, there is a vast majority of humanity which is sceptical, if not outright hostile, to the idea of Sai Baba being the Supreme Being. The idea of God incarnating Himself in flesh seems to be

i

equally unacceptable, if not outright repugnant, to the intellect of many behavioral scientists. Add to this the resistance many have to spirituality in general, and gurus, and Babas in particular. This at a time when we have been duped by a large number of charismatic spiritual figures from both East and West claiming a large following and extraordinary powers, yet in a while proving to have feet of clay, or worse. It is easy to see why the sophisticated intellectuals would be highly sceptical of yet another claim.

Millions in India and abroad are willing to accept Sai Baba's word that He is God for the simple reason that there is not, and cannot be, any possible test barring faith for such a phenomenon. They are like the multitudes, who for similar reasons, accepted the "Godword" of Christ, Zoroaster, Mohammed, Rama, Krishna and Buddha.

Others reject it or maintain a dignified neutrality in relation to a phenomenon they cannot understand. However, there was a minority led by Dr. H. Narasimhaiah, former Vice-Chancellor of Bangalore University, who mounted a campaign of calumnly against Baba. They insisted on Baba being subjected to "a proper empirical investigation under controlled conditions."

The detractors of Baba tried to play on the gullibility of the sceptics by asking: What is the need for God to take human form? Why the triple incarnation of Shirdi, Sathya and Prema Sai? Why did the task have to be divided into three separate incarnations? Did Shirdi Baba actually claim that He would be born eight years after His death in 1918? What made Sathya Sai Baba so sure that He was Shirdi Baba incarnated? What is the need for a God-man to demonstrate miracles like creating vibhuti and other trinkets which any magician can conjure? Isn't the gift of an Omega or HMT watch an act of cheating the company or breach of its patent? Why does He not materialise a pumpkin or a cucumber or a watch with a distinct mark to prove that it is a creation of His and not a transfer of somebody else's manufacture? If Baba is God, as He claims, why does He not help people in distress by bringing rains in times of drought, or creating food when there is famine, by His Sankalpa Shakti? Cannot an Avatar help humanity to control the natural forces and prevent calamities like earthquakes, floods, droughts, famines and epidemics? Why does He not submit himself to investigation under "controlled conditions?"

Russy Khursheed Karanjia, Editor-in-Chief of the widely read weekly tabloid BLITZ, has the rare distinction of having interviewed such a galaxy of world leaders as Nehru, Naseer, Khrushchov, Castro, Zhou Enlai, Arafat and the Shah of Iran. He travelled all the way to Puttaparthi in September 1976 to investigate the truth and seek answers to all the questions raised by Baba's detractors.

Karanjia employed his vast journalistic experience and skill to ask pointed questions to Baba on the issues raised by His critics during a no-holds barred, two and a half hour interview - the longest ever granted by Baba to any journalist. And, Baba effectively answered all these queries, and many more.

Russy came, saw and was conquered.

The interview, which forms the core of this book was published in four parts, and was a comprehensive exploration of Baba's mind, philosophy and technology. (Karanjia calls Baba a scientist of consciousness.) It will be of interest to the sceptics, as well as His devotees, for all times to come.

GOD LIVES IN INDIA

GOD LIVES IN INDIA. His contemporary Avatar rests in the trinity of Shirdi Baba, Sai Baba and Prema Baba to come. Sathya Sai Baba, the second of the triple incarnation, asserted in the course of a marathon interview, "In my present Avatar I have come armed with the fullness of the power of the formless God to save humanity."

This may appear to be an extraordinarily controversial claim to those unfamiliar with the spiritual depths of Hindu religio-philosophy. The latter totally accepts the Avatar concept which broadly means the descent of the Divine principle into human affairs. In the Bhagavad Gita, Lord Krishna intervenes to save humanity from evil forces. The Puranas personify Earth, the Mother, as groaning under a similar burden to supplicate God for relief.

SOLUTION & CURE TO WORLD'S ILLS

To Baba's devotees, the Avatar has similarly come to provide both the solution, and the cure, to a world living in terror of a nuclear holocaust. The false dichotomies created by Western thought between God and Man, Purusha and Deva, simply do not exist in Indian scriptures which prescribe the assimilation of God in man and man in God as the basis of religion.

Baba personifies this philosophy. As He told me, "God is man and man is God. All of us have something of God, the Divine spark, within us. All men are Divine like myself with the Spirit embodied in human flesh and bone. The only difference is that they are unaware of this Godhood."

For the doubting or confused minority to which section I then belonged, Swamiji has this message, "Those who want to secure pearls from the sea have to dive deep to fetch them. It does not

1

help them to dabble among the shallow waves near the shore and say that the sea has no pearls and all stories about them are false. Likewise, if a person wants to secure the love and grace of the Avatar, he must also dive deep and get submerged in Sai Baba. Then only will he become one with Me and carry Me in his innermost heart."

SPIRITUAL LOVE & GRACE

I have still not dived deep enough into this ocean of love and devotion to secure the grace. My experience of Baba is limited to a brief encounter in Bombay followed by the long dialogue at Puttaparthi. Nevertheless, the encounter was a fantastic, almost shattering one.

Swamiji discarded the high throne-like chair used for group darshans to come down and sit cross-legged with us - Dr. Bhagavantam, who acted as interpreter, Indulal Shah, my escort and myself - on the stone floor of a modest, unfurnished room for over two hours and a half.

Baba not only radiated powerful emanations of what I can describe as spiritual love and grace, but went on to amaze me with knowledge of the most intimate developments affecting my life and work. He appeared also to know beforehand the questions I had planned to ask. Soon as I began asking one, He would stop me with a gentle tap on the knee to begin answering it. I never completed a question. Still I got all the answers.

HAVEN OF SUPREME BLISS

Swamiji's Ashram, Prasanthi Nilayam, the Haven of Supreme Bliss, is fast assuming the status and symbol of a secular Vatican. It lives up to its calling. There is something psyche about it; a spiritual presence which casts its spell on the visitor. Simple but solemn rituals enhance its spirituality. I was awakened at four o' clock in the morning to join the Omkar ceremony in the austere

2

temple hall which soon reverberated to the thunder of a thousand throated Aum's.

As the thunder yielded to the silence of meditation, I could not help thinking what a mighty supersensory force could be created by a whole nation, city or village intoning Omkar the Prasanthi Nilayam way. It could move mountains and change the course of rivers. In olden times, it used to be employed to bring rain in times of drought and to command Nature herself.

The Omkar was followed by bhajans for which the Puttaparthi birds, waking with the dawn, orchestrated Nature's own musical accompaniment. By eight, thousands of people from far and near had collected in the temple courtyard for Baba's darshan.

Soon afterwards, the familiar dark and slender figure of middle height in a flaming orange robe and Afro hairstyle, around which His faithful see a bluish-white aura, emerged from His residence, and walked out to meet the assembly.

There was something ethereal about the figure as well as the walk. They say Baba incarnates the Shiva-Shakthi union in His body. He certainly embodies both masculinity and femininity. Krishna, as we read of Him in the scriptures, must have resembled Swamiji. His walk is that of a dancer floating in graceful movement.

IMAGE OF KRISHNA INCARNATION

As I watched Him going around the devotees, materialising vibhuti for the needful, He seemed to be there and not there at the same time. Sometimes He would appear to be talking or singing to Himself, at others waving His hand palm upwards in the air in rhythmic mudhras as it were.

The impact of contact between the devotees and their Bhagawan was immediate, electric and powerful. It was like the point-counter-point between musical instruments, or melodies

3

whose vibrations inspire newer and ever newer notes, until they merge into Divinity. Baba and the people seemed to resonate together in a telepathic dialogue of a spiritual intensity which has to be seen to be believed.

Even as I watched this drama, Baba was answering my suspicions, doubts and queries. Was He the patron Swamiji of the wealthy and the powerful few against the poor masses? No, He went first to the common people, most of them from the peasant stock. Next, He beckoned a few of them - a dozen men and another dozen women - to a private interview, helping them with His own hands into the room.

POOR CAME FIRST, RICH LAST

I watched the drama very closely. Those He chose were from the poorest and weakest sectors, some of them physically ill, and at least one mentally sick boy. I do not know what happened in the closed room, but from the look on their faces when they came out, they all seemed to be in a relaxed, happier condition.

Next, Baba came out to take me in together with Bhagavantam and Indulal Shah. I could not help looking back, for on the other side were seated a number of wealthy devotees. Some of them belonged to an industrial group devoted to Swamiji, which had lost the head of the family and whose widow had made Baba's Ashram her home. Yet, they had to wait through the two and a half hours of my interview.

So, the poor came first, the rich last. In the middle was I - a sceptic, a critic, a Marxist - who had in the past openly questioned and criticised Sathya Sai Baba.

BABA'S SPIRITUAL REVOLUTION

As Baba told me, His spiritual revolution is broadly based on the fundamentals of the three W's - WORK, WORSHIP and

4

WISDOM - in the context of the absolute equality of human brotherhood. Around me I found illustrations aplenty of this doctrine. The lady sweeping the courtyard was a former Maharani. The gentleman who attended to me was a Magistrate who had resigned from judicial service to join the Ashram. The interpreter between Baba and myself used to be India's foremost scientist. Need I say more?

The interview that follows is a comprehensive exploration of Baba's mind, philosophy and technology (for He is a scientist of consciousness) which ran through four issues of BLITZ. The first part deals with the holy mission and Divine purpose of Swamiji's triple incarnation which, in brief, is to create through His evangel of love a brotherhood of mankind, and to save the world from a nuclear holocaust. The second part provides the educational and socio-economic methodology of this spiritual revolution through Baba's 3,000 or so educational and social service institutions designed to evolve a new race of Godmen. In the third part, Sai Baba answers His critics. In the final section, Baba reveals the relevance of His Avatarhood to contemporary times.

* * *

Now to the text of the interview......

Q: At the outset, Swamiji, we would like to know something about your triple incarnation - past, present and future - that is, from Shirdi Sai Baba to Sathya Sai Baba and the Prema Sai Baba to come, according to Your prophecy?

Baba: First of all, you must grasp the complete Oneness of the three incarnations of contemporary times with those of the past, like Rama and Krishna. This is a difficult task. When people cannot understand the present, how can they comprehend the past? Every incarnation is full and complete in relation to the time, the environment and the task. There is no distinction between the various appearances of God as Rama, Krishna or Sai.

5

Rama came to feed the roots of Truth and Righteousness. Krishna followed to foster the plant of Peace and Love. Now, these sacred principles are in danger of wholesale destruction by reason of human weakness under the onslaught of evil forces. They are overcoming the good, the spiritual and the Divine in man. That is why the present Avatar has come invested with the totality of Cosmic power to save Dharma from anti-Dharma.

WHY GOD TAKES HUMAN FORM

Q: By the present Avatar, You mean Sai Baba?

Baba: Yes, I incarnate from age to age, time to time, to save Dharma from anti-Dharma. Whenever strife, discord and disharmony overwhelm the world, God incarnates in human form to show mankind the way to love, harmony and peace.

Q: That is understandable. But sceptics wonder why God should assume a human form?

Baba: Because that is the only way to incarnate the God within man. The Avatar takes the human form and behaves in a human way so that humanity can feel kinship with Divinity. At the same time, He rises to godly heights, so that mankind, also, can aspire to reach God. The realisation of the indwelling God as the motivator of life is the task for which Avatars come in human form.

Previous Avatars like Rama and Krishna had to destroy a few individuals who could be identified as enemies of the godly way of life, and thus restore the dharmic path. Today, however, wickedness has tainted so many that humanity itself, stands under the threat of destruction. Therefore, in my present Avatar, I have come armed with the fullness of the power of the formless God to correct mankind, raise human consciousness, and put people back on the right path of Truth, Righteousness, Peace and Love to Divinity.

MESSAGE OF TRIPLE INCARNATION

Q: Why did this task have to be divided into the three separate incarnations of Shirdi, Sathya and Prema Baba?

Baba: They are not separate. I have already mentioned the complete Oneness of the three in the final objective of the mission. I will give you an example. Take a kilo of *Gur* (candy). The whole of it tastes sweet. Next, break it into small pieces. Each of them is sweet. Finally, break them further into small grains. You find the same sweetness in them. So, the difference is one of quantity and not quality. It is the same with the Avatars. Their tasks and powers requisite to them differ according to the time, the situation and the environment, but they belong to and derive from, one and the same Dharma Swarup or Divine Body.

Let us take the example of fruit. It begins with the seed which grows into the TREE and from it comes fruit. Work can be compared to the seed, worship to the tree, and wisdom to the fruit.

The previous Avatar, Shirdi Baba, laid the base for secular integration, and gave mankind the message of Duty, that is, WORK. The mission of the present Avatar is to make everybody realise that since the same God or Divinity resides in everyone, people should respect, love and help each other irrespective of caste, colour or creed. Thus, every WORK can become an act of WORSHIP. Finally Prema Sai, the third Avatar, shall promote the evangel that not only does God reside in everybody, but everyone himself is God. That will be the final WISDOM which will enable every man and woman to rise to be God. Thus, the three Avatars carry the triple message of WORK, WORSHIP and WISDOM.

MAN MUST DEVELOP INTO MANKIND

Q: So, what are, in sum, the holy mission and Divine purpose of this triple incarnation?

Baba: To unite all mankind into one caste or family with the establishment of the Divinity - that is, Atmic reality - in every man or woman, which is the basis on which the entire Cosmic design rests. Once this is realised, the common Divine heritage that binds man to man and man to God will become apparent, and Love shall prevail as the guiding light of the Universe.

In the first place, MAN has to develop into MANKIND in the fullness of its integrated potential. At present mankind as such is absent in the world. There is no synthesis between thought, word and deed. Man today thinks one thing, says something different, and acts quite the contrary. So, what we have is the individual man confused, confounded and bombarded with contradictory thoughts. What we do not see is MANKIND in him, motivated by good thoughts, good words and good deeds. We have to make him realise God within him to develop a synthesis correlating thought, word and deed.

Once this primary lesson is taught in the family, the school, the college, the society, the cities, the states, and the nations of the world, man will become conscious of the fact that all mankind belongs to one family. As Christ preached, all are one, be alike to everyone. The vital issue is the ONENESS: one caste, one class, one creed of humanity and this can be achieved only by the surrender of one's self or ego to pure, selfless, universal love and devotion. Love is the basis, the common denominator, and devotion the Divine spark, the cementing, unifying, integrating factor between man and man, and man and God.

Let me give you an illustration. (Baba spreads His handkerchief on the ground between us). Here is a piece of cloth. As you see, it is all made of threads. Pull out the threads separately, and the cloth becomes weak. Put them together, and it is firm and strong. It is the same with mankind. Love binds it like the million, billion threads in cloth, and Devotion reunites it with God. I always

8

say, 'Start the day with love. Fill the day with love. End the day with love. This is the quickest way, the surest path to God.'

Life is love, enjoy it;

Life is a challenge, meet it;

Life is a song, sing it;

Life is a dream, realise it;

Life is game, play it.

SHIRDI BABA INCARNATE

Q: Did Shirdi Baba actually claim that He would be born eight years after His death in 1918?

Baba: Yes, He did. This has been recorded by Kaka Dikshit as well as a number of other devotees who were with Shirdi Baba.

Q: What makes You so sure that You are Shirdi Baba incarnate?

Baba: The knowledge of My own authentic experience, of course. Since no one who knew Shirdi Baba is alive today, there is no evidence except My own knowledge and experience. The very fact that I announced that I am Shirdi Baba 40 years ago, when I was 10 and when nobody in this part of the South had known, or even heard of, Shirdi Baba, proves this fact.

DHARMA ALONE CAN SAVE WORLD

Q: The existing situation where humanity is being driven by evil forces to destruction, as you have correctly analysed it, appears to suggest the inevitability of another Mahabharata-type war. Does

9

this mean that the salvation for which You are working can be consummated only after a destructive war?

Baba: The evil must and shall be removed before such a catastrophe takes place. There will be minor wars and skirmishes, of course. These cannot be helped in the existing state of affairs. The Mahabharata was a different issue altogether. Lord Krishna decreed it, and in fact, led Arjuna as his Divine Charioteer to the battlefield in order to rid the world of evil men and ungodly forces.

Today, as I told you, the evil is so widespread that humanity itself would be destroyed in a nuclear holocaust in the event of a world war. It is to prevent such a catastrophe that this Avatar has come to raise human consciousness above the existing syndrome of anger, hate, violence and war, and to save the world from disaster. This can be achieved only by the re-establishment of the brotherhood of mankind through the Vedas, Shastras and all religions with their evangel of Dharma to liberate the human race from the chains of Karma.

I always say, 'Let the different faiths exist, let them flourish, let the glory of God be sung in all the languages in a variety of tunes.' That should be the ideal. Respect the differences between the faiths, and recognize them as valid so far as they do not extinguish the flame of Unity.

GOD IS MAN MINUS DESIRE

Q: From what Baba has said, it seems there is not much difference or dichotomy between God and man. Am I right?

Baba : Quite right. God is man and man is God. All of us have something of God, the Divine spark, within us. All men are Divine like Myself, but with the Spirit embodied in human flesh and bone. The only difference is that they are unaware of this Godhood. They have come into this karmic prison through the mistakes of many lives. I have taken this mortal form out of My own freewill. They are bound to the body, while I am free of this bondage. The main difference is that they are shoved hither and thither by DESIRE, but I have no desire except the supreme one to make them DESIRELESS.

Take a paddy of rice by way of an illustration. Every grain of rice is enclosed in a husk. You have to remove the husk to get the grain of rice. Now husk and rice, both come from the same seed. Rice is the equivalent to God in man, while the husk can be compared to desire which reduces God to man. Therefore, My formula is:

Life + Desire = Man

Life - Desire = God

THE WAY TO SELF - REALISATION

Q: In what way can life without desire make Gods of men?

Baba: Life without desire means the realisation of the pure genuine Self that is Atma. Bound to desire, the Self degenerates into selfishness. Atma turns into ego. The way to Self-realisation is to cleanse the Self of this ego of selfishness. Then you reach a state of consciousness beyond the mind or intellect, revealing the true Self that is God. The mind is like a cloth that covers and stifles consciousness, the threads of which are desires. If we give up the desires, the threads fall, and the cloth disappears revealing our true nature. This is what the Vedanta means when it enjoins that one must get rid of the ego to realise Oneself.

Q: You mean that the mind of man, as such, creates the block between man and God?

Baba: Yes. One must make a distinction between the mind that is the ego, and the real Self that is consciousness. The latter

11

helps us to cross the frontiers of the ego-mind and become aware of Oneself as the witness of Truth. Normally, the scientist of the mind looks outside to what can be perceived by the senses existing in the world of the mind to ask, 'WHAT IS THIS?' The scientist of consciousness, on the other hand, always looks insides to that which is beyond the senses or the grasp of the mind to ask, 'WHAT IS THAT?'

One has, therefore, to rise beyond the mind to consciousness to achieve Self-realisation. To gain the infinite, universal Atma, the embodied Self must break out of the puny, finite little prison of individuality. Desire belongs to the senses, the brain, the mind; once you become free of it, you realise the Self, Atma, consciousness, enlightenment, and become one with the Cosmic Power. Self-realisation is God-realisation. THUS MAN REACHES GOD.

SYMBOL OF LOVE & DIVINITY

Q: What is the significance of the vibhuti and the trinkets that You materialise and gift to people? Is there any need for a God-man to demonstrate such miracles which any magician can conjure?

Baba: So far as I am concerned, this is evidence of My Divinity. All performances of magic, as you know, are done for the sake of income. These are tricks of the magician's trade. They constitute a kind of legalised cheating, the transfer of an object from one place to another by a trick of the hand which goes unnoticed. They involve no siddhi or miraculous power.

What I do is quite a different act of creation. It is neither magic, nor is it siddhi power. For one thing, I seek no return. For another, I do not cheat people by transferring objects, but I create them. Again, I do so not because of any need or desire of exhibition of My powers. For Me, this is a kind of visiting card to convince

12

people of My love for them and secure their devotion in return. Since love is formless, I use materialisation as evidence of My love. It is merely a symbol.

TALISMAN OF PROTECTION

Q: Still, I do not understand why you should materialise rings, bracelets, watches and those kind of trinkets?

Baba: Most people desire talismans symbolic of My protection, so I provide them. When they are in trouble, they FEEL the grip of the ring, bracelet or watch to remember Me, and call Me to their rescue, so that I can help them. On the other hand, if I give them something that they cannot wear, they are likely to store it and forget about it.

The main thing is that these trinkets or talismans, by whatever name you call them, give people a sense of security and protection they need in time of trouble or crisis, and create a symbolic link covering the long distances between them and Myself. When the devotees need Me, these objects flash the message as if by wireless, and I instantly come to their rescue.

Q: I am sorry to be so persistent, Swamiji, but isn't the gift of an Omega or HMT watch an act of cheating the company or a breach of its patent?

Baba: I assure you there is no such thing. It would be cheating the company or breaching the patent if it was a case of transfer of the watch from one place or the other, but I do not transfer. I totally create. Whatever I Will, instantly materialises. I know of no company that has complained about any breach of patent.

SIGNIFICANCE OF VIBHUTI

Q: What about the vibhuti materialised by You? We would like to know its relevance because Your critics are trying to

13

discredit You by sending around magicians who produce exact replicas of vibhuti?

Baba: What I materialise is a manifestation of Divinity with a potent significance as well as symbolisation. It is symbolic of the cosmic, immortal and infinite nature of all forms of God, Atma or the Spirit - that is, what is left when everything worldly, transient and changeable has burnt away.

I have spoken to you of the imperative of a desireless life. After Shiva had burnt the God of Desire, Kama, into a heap of ashes, He adorned Himself with the ash to shine as the conqueror of desire. When Kama was destroyed, Prema reigned as the Goddess of Love. Such is the significance of ash.

In the first place, it is symbolic of the life-death cycle in which everything ultimately reduces itself to ash. 'For dust thou art, and unto dust shalt thou returnest.' Ash, or dust, is the final condition of things. It cannot undergo any further change. In the spiritual context, it constitutes a warning to the receiver to give up desire, to burn all passions, attachments and temptations in the fire of worship which makes one pure in thought, word and deed.

It is in order to press home this lesson that I materialise ash for those who come to me with love and devotion. Like the other materialisations, it also acts as a talisman healing the sick and giving protection to those who need it. It is the symbol of Divinity, quite different from the magician's trickery mentioned by you.

MIRACLES OF HEALING

Q: You are believed to have performed miraculous cures to the extent of resurrecting the dead. There are cases where You reportedly have saved people from drowning and other accidents in distant places. Medical experts have attested to remote-controlled surgical operations performed by You. How do You manage these?

Baba: By My own Sankalpa - that is, Divine will and power. As an Avatar, this power is intrinsic, inherent, total and natural to My will and decision. I need no tantra and no yantra to perform the so-called miracles which are natural to My state. My powers are simply the expression or assertion of the reality of godliness which merges Me with everything, everywhere, at all times and places. The miracles belong to the boundless power of God.

Now coming to the main points of your question, this healing phenomenon has a dual aspect. I can cure, save, even resurrect people provided they are in a spiritually receptive condition. It is like the positive and negative currents of electricity. My capacity to heal can be compared to the positive current. Your devotion to Me is the negative current. Once the two come together, the devotion provides what is called the miracle of healing.

It is man's mind that is really responsible for his illness or health. He himself is the cause or motivator of either. So when it comes to healing or curing, the necessary faith has to be created within his mind for the purpose. All I do is to invest him with the confidence, will and power to cure himself. It is My abounding love reciprocated by the intensity of the devotees faith in Me that produces the desired result.

NOT SIDDHIS, NOR MAGICAL TRICKS

Q: So these are not siddhic powers or magical tricks, as Your critics suggest?

Baba: They are neither magical tricks nor siddhic powers. These can come to everybody with the appropriate discipline and yoga exercises, but My powers to protect, heal and save people and materialise objects originate in God, and can be used only by an Avatar. They are in no way designed, disciplined or developed, but flow from Cosmic Power itself.

Q: Some say that You command invisible Spirits which can transfer objects from one place to another on Your orders?

Baba: There is no need for Me to command invisible Spirits since My own Divine will materialises the objects. I am everything, everywhere, omniscient, omnipotent and omnipresent; and so whatever I Will instantly happens. Like the qualities of truth, love and peace, these are things that generate the Atmic or Cosmic forces behind the Universe.

THE INDWELLING GOD

Q: Your followers in India as well as abroad claim positive evidence of the presence of Baba in their innermost hearts. Some have written of You as their indwelling God. What is the explanation of this phenomenon?

Baba: This is the grace begotten of My love for them reciprocated by their devotion. After all, as I repeatedly say, we all belong to the same Divine Principle. The Godliness which is present in everybody in the form of a little spark exists in Me as the full flame, and it is My mission to develop every little spark of God in everyone to the fullness of the Divine flame.

The first imperative of this development is that the receiver of the grace also provides from his or her side the devotion necessary to the consummation. Those who carry the presence of Baba in their hearts like an indwelling God belong to this kind of devotee. They come to Me, see Me and hear Me, experience My love for them and receive it with devotion. Thus, they become part of Me and my Divinity.

To the doubting or confused ones, I give this illustration. Those who want to secure pearls from the sea have to dive deep to fetch them. It does not help them to dabble among the shallow waves near the shore and say that the sea has no pearls and all stories

16

about them are false. Likewise, if a person wants to secure the love and grace of this Avatar, he must also dive deep and get submerged in Sai Baba. Then only will he become one with Me, and carry Me in his innermost heart.

Q: The critics of Swamiji ask why Sai Baba does not help people in distress by bringing rains in times of drought or creating food where there is famine by means of His Sankalpa Shakti? Cannot an Avatar help humanity to control the natural force and prevent calamities like earthquakes, floods, droughts, famine and epidemics?

The answers to these and other questions are published in the next chapter.

SAI BABA'S SPIRITUAL SOCIALISM

Sathya Sai Baba revealed Himself as a scientist of consciousness, showing mankind the way to incarnate the indwelling God with love, devotion, detachment and desirelessness and to evolve to a higher level of enlightenment in the first part of this interview.

His supremacy in the field of this lost science is well and widely recognized. The noted American physician and psychiatrist, Samuel H. Sandweiss, MD, has paid Him the finest professional tribute by giving psychiatry the new calling of "SAI-CHIATRY" after Baba.

In the sections that follow, Baba employs His "SAI-CHIATRY" to add an entirely new spiritual dimension to the evolutionary, as well as socio-economic, science which might inspire a "Sandweiss" in this field to rename it "SAI-ENCE."

MISSION TO REMAKE MANKIND

Baba's holy mission, as stated in the dialogue that follows, leads the reader deep into the spiritual significance of the Cosmic drama. It is, first of all, to UNMAKE the materialist, ego-bound man, and next to REMAKE him in the image and likeness of God.

This new God-man armed with Sankalpa Shakti Divine power will transcend the Karmic laws and command the Natural forces to avert calamities like drought, flood, famine and earthquake.

In the socio-economic field also, Baba offers a spiritual solution whereby the wealthy and the poor will be joined in a co-operative working partnership. Here again, both the classes will be UNMADE and REMADE by Baba's love and grace so that the rich will sacrifice their wants to enable the poor to secure their needs.

KARMIC ROLE IN COSMIC DRAMA

Here is the text of the interview:

Q: Critics of Sai Baba ask why an Avatar armed with Sankalpa Shakti - that is, Divine power - does not help people in distress by bringing rains in times of drought or creating food grains when there is famine? Cannot Baba help humanity to control the natural forces and prevent calamities like earthquakes, floods, droughts, famine and epidemics?

Baba: This is precisely what I am doing by incarnating the indwelling God in man to overcome such calamities. There are two ways in which an Avatar can help people, an instant solution as against a long term one.

Any instant solution would go against the fundamental quality of Nature itself, as well as the Karmic Law of cause and effect. Most people live in the material world of their desires and egos which is governed by this Law. They reap the fruits of their actions. This brings about their evolution or devolution. If the Avatar intervenes to instantly solve their problems, it would stop all action, development, even evolution. This solution can be ruled out because it totally negates the natural laws.

The other and more effective alternative presents a longterm solution whereby the Avatar leads the people themselves to a higher level of consciousness to enable them to understand the truth of spiritual laws, so that they may turn towards righteousness, and steadfastly work for better conditions. This will relate them back to Nature and the Karmic Law of Causation. They would then transcend the cycle of cause and effect in which today they are involved as victims, and thereby command and control the natural forces to be able to avert the calamities you mention.

RAISING MAN TO GOD

Q: You mean that You are presently raising the consciousness of mankind to a godlike condition to enable them to command their own destiny?

Baba: Exactly. They will become shareholders of My Sankalpa Shakti (Divine power, universal energy). I have to work through them to a higher reality in order to enable them to master the natural laws and forces. If I cure everything instantly, leaving the people at their present level of consciousness, they would soon mess up things and be at one another's throats again with the result that the same chaotic situation would develop in the world.

Suffering and misery are the inescapable acts of the Cosmic drama. God does not decree these calamities, but man invites them by way of retribution for his own evil deeds. This is corrective punishment which induces mankind to give up the wrong path and return to the right path, so that he may experience the godlike condition of Sat-Chit-Ananda - that is, an existence of wisdom and bliss. All this is part of the grand synthesis in which the negatives serve to glorify the positives. Thus, death glorifies immortality, ignorance glorifies wisdom, misery glorifies bliss, night glorifies dawn.

So, finally, if the Avatar brings the calamities mentioned by you to an immediate end, which I can and do when there is a great need, the whole drama of creation with its Karmic (universal, inescapable duty) Law will collapse. Remember, these calamities occur not because of what God has made of man, but really because of what man has made of man. Therefore, man has to be unmade and remade with his ego destroyed and replaced by a transcendent consciousness, so that he may rise above the Karmic cycle to command Nature and avert its calamities. This is the work of the Avatar which I am presently doing.

A CO-OPERATIVE BROTHERHOOD

Q: Dr. V.K. Gokak, former Vice-Chancellor of Bangalore University, has described your socio-economic experiment as "the revolution of revolutions," transforming the individual as well as society as a whole. Would you explain the methodology as well as the machinery of this revolution?

Baba: I have no methodology or machinery in the accepted organizational sense. My methodology is a simple one based on conversion by love, and the machinery is one of human co-operation and brotherhood again deriving from love. What we need today are one single caste of humanity, one common religion of love, and one universal language of the heart. This is the simple methodology or machinery through which both the individual and society can be transformed.

So the basis of the change is individual transformation through love. Love is My instrument and merchandise. Whatever I do in the field of sociology or economics is sought to be done by and through love. Both the wealthy and the poor who want Me can come to Me only on a basis of absolute equality, and I use them to synthesise the existing socio-economic contradictions into a co-operative brotherhood.

FUSION OF RICH WITH POOR

Q: Have you succeeded in bringing about this synthesis, Swamiji, particularly with the wealthy and powerful classes?

Baba: I have not reached them all as a class, but to the extent that I am able to contact them individually, the results are encouraging. The wealthy and powerful, of course, present a difficult problem in the matter of transformation. They need a special approach. The poorer people, on the other hand, are very co-operative. They understand, appreciate and help My plans and ideas.

21

Q: What is Your solution to this escalating conflict between wealth and power on one side and poverty and weakness on the other?

Baba: The transformation of both into a single co-operative brotherhood in terms of equality without competition or conflict. This can result only from Truth and Love. The main issue is to fuse the two classes into one single class. The problem, however, is one of bringing them together on a common base or platform. Wealthy people live isolated in a certain state or condition. The poor also are similarly isolated in another state or condition. How do we bring them together?

I do so in many subtle ways by breaking the barriers of wealth and poverty and creating a feeling of equality and oneness between the poor and the rich. In this Ashram (spiritual community), you find them living and working together, even performing menial labour on terms of complete equality. Here, there are no distinctions whatever, not any special facilities for the rich. They live, eat, work, worship and sleep like the poor. All live like a community of workers to share the common austerities of the Ashram.

Despite our rigorous discipline, industrialists and businessmen want to come here. Why? Because they secure peace of mind beyond physical comfort which no wealth, or power on Earth, can purchase or provide.

Thus, we open to them a wonderful new world of spiritual treasures, and they must sacrifice material wants and comforts. My mission is to show them the way to the peace of mind which everybody, poor and rich alike, desires. In that process of spiritual evolution, the seeker learns that this blissful state cannot be purchased for money in a shop, or gifted to one by anybody but oneself. It can come only from the universal source of Divinity, the indwelling God, that embraces poor and rich alike.

This concept creates a common fellowship, a brotherhood of give and take, between the wealthy and the poor. Those who have too much are obliged to give up their unnecessary wants while those who have too little get their needs fulfilled.

After all, in spiritual terms, all mankind belongs to one and the same class, caste or religion. The Divine principles in each and all of them derive from one and the same God. This fundamental Oneness has to be made manifest to them through direct contact with spiritual realities and the persuasive expanding power of love, until they become part of the Universal religion of Work, Worship and Wisdom.

MATERIAL WEALTH IS SPIRITUAL POVERTY

Q: All this would be a simple and welcome evangel for the poor since they lose nothing and gain everything from Your philosophy, but what about the rich who would have to lose all if they followed it?

Baba: That is the crux of the problem. They simply have to lose, surrender, and submerge their false values if they want My grace. So long as people continue to be slaves to materialistic definitions of wealth and poverty, there can be no solution. I, therefore, try to convert their minds and hearts to spiritual values and truths.

After all, who is the richest man? One who has the largest wants, and therefore, troubles and worries? Or, one who is satisfied with the barest necessities of life, and therefore, is more or less desireless and comparatively happy? Judged from this criterion of happiness, the poor are spiritually rich while the rich are spiritually poor. It is not material, but spiritual satisfaction, that ultimately makes life worth living.

As I have said before, life without desire brings Divinity to man, and those who seek My grace must shed desire and greed.

23

Riches provide a fatal temptation. They are the source and cause of human bondage. The desire to raise the standard of life can never be satisfied. It leads to multiplication of wants and consequent troubles and frustrations.

The solution lies in our emphasis on the quality as the standard of life, on high thinking and lowly living. The mind is the horse, the body the cart; to achieve mental peace, you must put the horse of high thinking before the cart of physical comfort.

MONEY - MIND BONDAGE

Q: This is sound philosophy but how do you implement it in action?

Baba: The rich as well as the poor come to Sai Baba to seek love, peace and liberation from their problems or troubles. My prescription to them is absolute selflessness and desirelessness. To the poor, this is a natural state or condition. So My love flows to them to embrace their devotion. Thus they obtain My grace. The rich, on the other hand, cannot secure this grace without surrendering their materialistic outlook and selfish attachments. So it becomes obligatory for them to sacrifice material greed to receive spiritual grace. I tell them, 'Ego lives by getting and forgetting, Love lives by giving and forgiving.' In this way, I change their mental attitude. I transform their monkey-minds into loving, giving and forgiving minds.

Q: Monkey-minds? Baba what do you mean?

Baba: It is a kind of mentality that is used by the peasants to trap and destroy monkeys. When the peasant wants to catch a monkey, he uses a big pot with a narrow mouth as a trap. Inside the pot, he puts edibles which the monkey loves. The monkey finds the pot, and puts its paws inside it to grasp as much of the stuff as he can hold. Once it does so, it is unable to pull out its paws from the small mouth of the pot. It imagines that someone inside the pot is holding its paws, so it struggles and attempts to run away with the pot, only to fail and get trapped. No one is holding the monkey; it has trapped itself because of its greed. If only it lets the stuff in its paws go, it will be free of the bondage.

In the same way, I tell the rich people, man is tempted by the wealth, pleasures and desires of the world. When he gets lost in such attachment and suffers the consequences of greed, he thinks that something is binding him down, capturing him, destroying him. He does not realise that he himself is responsible for this bondage to the monkey-mind and can liberate himself.

BABA'S SPIRITUAL SOCIALISM

Q: Baba seems to be prescribing a kind of spiritual socialism based on the conversion of wealth into a trusteeship for the removal of poverty?

Baba: Yes, a trusteeship based on love, cooperation and brotherhood. What else can one do? The change must evolve from the heart; it cannot be imposed from the outside. All materialist doctrines have failed to bring about any real transformation. There is no equality anywhere. Only spiritual transformation to a desireless mentality can put through the imperative revolution in human consciousness from which alone the desired changes can accrue.

We need to transform society from false to real values. We have to convince people that the ideal of a high standard of life is wrong. It must be replaced with a high level of living and thinking on the basis of humility, morality, compassion and detachment, as against the existing greed for competitive luxury and conspicuous consumption. People have to be convinced that the only way to rouse the latent Divinity in them is to master desires and conquer greed for pleasure and luxury, instead of being a slave to these false materialistic values.

25

SAI PATH TO DHARMA (RIGHTEOUSNESS)

Q: Then I take it that the various educational and social service organisations run by Baba - some 3,000 in all - are designed to create the cadres necessary for bringing about the desired socio-economic change by means of love and persuasion?

Baba: They are designed to put the new generation on the Sai Path of Truth, Righteousness, Peace, Love and Non-violence. Their motto - work is worship and duty is God - seeks to bring in the new social order related to Sathya - that is, Truth and Dharma - namely, Right Action.

SOCIOECONOMIC SYNTHESIS

Q: India has been described as a rich country of poor people. We have the wealth of the whole world locked up in the bosom of our good earth, and yet the people remain economically poor and backward. Have You any solution to rehabilitate our economy?

Baba: Your analysis is correct. The solution to the problem you have posed lies in hard work and increased production on a cooperative basis. To achieve this, one has to rid the people of the diseases of individuality, greed and selfishness. Every individual must be taught to think and work in the broader concept of society and its needs. Once that is done, there will be less talk, more work.

Here again, it is the spiritual path that can save this country, and the world, from the wrongs of a materialistic order. What we need is a synthesis of the spiritual and material aspects of life. That will provide man with the social conscience and cooperative spirit imperative to the creation of national wealth and prosperity through selfless, cooperative labour.

DESIRE MUST BE EQUALIZED

Q: Very good counsel, Swamiji, but the trouble is that all the wealth created by labour appears to find its way into the pockets of a rich and powerful minority. Have You a spiritual prescription for this inequality?

Baba: There is no doubt that the distribution is not taking place properly. The existing doctrines of equality, socialism, etc., have not succeeded in achieving equality in distribution of wealth and property. The difficulty is that you can equalise wealth, land and property by legistation, but can the law bring about equality in the desires of the people? This requires the healing touch of spiritualism.

To begin with, one has to curb desire and its evil consequences. We must persuade the rich that desire and its fulfillment in materialistic wants is an aspect of the monkey-mind which can only harm them and put them under bondage. This alone will solve the problem of inequality and maldistribution. The rich will give up their extravagant wants, the poor will get what they need and a little more, and this process will bring more equitable distribution.

LESSER LUGGAGE : BETTER JOURNEY

Q: To conclude this section, Swamiji, would You sum up the main causes of India's social and economic backwardness?

Baba: From a purely material viewpoint, it is a question of supply and demand. Because of the overpowering material values of our society, the demand is growing large, while the supply decreases. Then, of course, there is the problem of growing population. This triangular issue of economic imbalance needs to be spiritualised if an effective solution is to be found.

It is here that our insistence on a desireless life, in which human wants are reduced to the minimum needs comes to the rescue as the only possible way of restoring the social and economic balance. Curb your desires, reduce your wants, live in spiritual austerity, and the available material will be sufficient for all humanity. More than that, the tensions of a competitive socio-economic system will be dissolved, and peace of mind will be restored.

Life is like a journey in a vehicle between birth and death. The body is the vehicle in which you are motoring to death. The less luggage you carry the better. Why encumber yourself with worldly riches and material comforts when you may have to change your course, or even meet with some dislocation or accident, and in any case, at the end of the journey will have to leave behind all your possessions except your Atma? Would it not be better to attend to the immortal spirit rather than waste time, which is running out, on gaining wealth and securing comforts? This is the logic of spiritualism with which I seek to change the attitude of people.

THE AGONY OF NATARAJ

Shiva's glory in the Nataraj dance is matched by the agony involved in the Cosmic drama of creation, preservation and destruction symbolized by its steps and rhythms. Sathya Sai Baba, who has been explaining to BLITZ His mission to resurrect mankind to play their Godlike role in this drama, eloquently projects this agony as well as the glory in one of His characteristic poems.

I am Dance Master;

I am Nataraj, Prince of dancers.

You are all My pupils.

I alone know the agony

Of teaching you each step

to the dance.

"Baba's agony is humanity's agony," writes Charles Penn, His Australian biographer, and the Avatar corroborates this devotee's concept with the authenticity of his own personal experience. To one who carries the burden of human agony as well as glory, campaigns of calumny such as the one mounted by Dr. H. Narasimhaiah (former Vice-Chancellor of Bangalore University) and company could hurt less than a pinprick. Baba is least offended or concerned.

REASON CANNOT TEST TRANSCENDENCE

"It is only the fruit-laden tree that invites stones from the passersby," He told me in good humour with compassion lighting His eyes. "They cannot understand because we (they and I) function at two different levels of consciousness. How can reason test transcendence?" Throughout the last portion of the dialogue dealing with His detractors, Baba assumes this attitude of enlightened forgiveness.

"Assumes" probably conveys the wrong sense. To Baba, it comes simply and naturally as forgiveness toward the ignorant. Some presumption! I can almost hear Dr. Narasimhaiah fuming at the very association of Baba with God or Christ. Nevertheless, the claim and its rejection bring us to the gut issue of the whole controversy: either you accept Baba's word that He is God, or you condemn Him as a fraud.

Millions in India and abroad are willing to accept His word for the simple reason that there is not, and cannot be, any possible test, barring faith, for such a phenomenon. They are like the millions who, for the identical reason, accepted the "God Word" of Christ, Zoroaster, Mohammed, Buddha and Krishna.

Others either reject it or maintain a dignified neutrality in relation to a phenomenon they cannot comprehend. That is perfectly all right; each one to his own faith and conscience. But, there was a minority led by Dr. Narasimhaiah who insisted on making a public issue of their rejection. They further insisted on Baba being subjected to "a proper empirical investigation under controlled conditions."

FRAUD OF EMPIRICAL INVESTIGATION

This on the face of it was an absurd proposition. First of all, the Investigation Committee was not at all equipped with the requisite laboratory and sophisticated instruments imperative for the tests, let alone this transcendental phenomenon. Anyone who knows how such tests are carried on in the United States or the Soviet Union will realise that no "empirical test" is possible in India.

Earlier, when Pundit Gopi Krishna offered his kundalini arousal phenomenon to a similar clinical test, I had occasion to investigate this matter in cooperation with Dr. Karan Singh, the then Union Minister of Health and the All-India Institute of Medical Science at New Delhi. We found that anything resembling a proper examination needed an entire laboratory for neurophysiological investigation, computerised data processing and acquisition, metabolic and hormonal investigations and the Soviet discovery of Kirlian photography. This fact is on record in the Kundalini Project Report issued by the AIIMS.

So, a scientific investigation of the Baba phenomenon being impossible, what were the tests in the mind of Dr. Narsimhiah? He told a colleague (Janardhan Thakur of Sunday, Calcutta: September. 5, 1976): "Well, perhaps we may have to ask Baba to take off His gown. What about His hair? It may be fake. Some say it is. We have to find out. Perhaps we would have to use metal detectors, as is done with smugglers..."

RIDICULOUS & INSULTING

These so-miscalled "tests" seemed grotesquely ridiculous and grossly insulting on the face of them. Just imagine, "...as is done with smugglers...!" Janardhan Thakur writes that on Dr. Narasimhaiah's advice, and with Baba's consent, he actually pulled His hair "hard, really hard" to find it was real. Baba even parted His hair with His hand to show him the roots. When he apologized for the outrage, Baba only smiled, "Never mind, you are a good investigator."

Expectedly, BLITZ and I came under similar vilification. I was supposed to have been bribed, bought, hypnotized, converted or otherwise influenced by Baba. One person went to the limit of questioning my use of titles like Baba or Swamiji. After all, His name is Baba! Did they expect me to change it? And, Swamiji is a respectful way of calling any ordinary Sadhu or religious person.

31

LET READERS JUDGE....

The only crime committed by your journal and its writers was to go to Puttaparthi with a neutral, open mind. No journalist who has taken leave of his senses can afford to ignore a phenomenon like Sathya Sai Baba. So, when the controversy started with Dr. Narasimhaiah's challenge, we featured it as: "Sai Baba... Fraud or God?" (Blitz: July, '51), giving both sides. Our Bangalore correspondent interviewed both Baba and Narasimhaiah. In fact, Narasimhaiah got the bigger coverage; "How can God be so unsure of Himself? (August. 21). Simultaneously, both eyewitness reports as well as complaints appeared in several issues (August 14 to 28).

Finally, to the suggestion of both His devotees and adversaries, I myself went to Puttaparthi to put all available criticisms straight to Baba and obtain His answers. As I have already admitted, the encounter was a fantastic, almost shattering one. That did not mean, however, that I had been bribed, bought, hypnotised, converted or otherwise influenced. I had only sought to interpret Baba's philosophy and mission in an objective, albeit sympathetic, manner suspending my own judgement, so that every individual is left free to make his decision according to his faith and conscience. The purpose of this series is to place the thoughts of this extraordinary phenomenon before the readers to enable them to make their own judgement.

WHY NO PUMPKINS OR CUCUMBER

Here is the last portion of the interview:

Q: Baba has already clarified most of the issues raised by Dr. Narasimhaiah, who asks why You do not materialise a pumpkin or cucumber or a watch with a distinct mark to prove that it is Your creation and not a transfer of somebody else's manufacture?

Baba: Pumpkins and cucumbers can be materialised as easily as rings or objects, but these are perishable objects, and the whole point of materialisation, as I have already explained, lies in their permanence. That is why rings or watches become more serviceable as talismans, or means of contact and communication between the Avatar and His devotees.

The point they are trying to make out is that big objects like pumpkins cannot be transferred while small ones like rings can be. But, as I have repeatedly said, I do not transfer things by a sleight of hands, I create them by way of talisman. Now, coming to your question about a ring or watch with a distinct mark to prove that it is my own creation, would you like me to materialise something for you?

MIRACLE OF OM RING

Q: Yes, Swamiji, I certainly would.

Baba: He waved His hand in the air to produce a silver ring bearing the inscription of 'OM' in the centre with 'Sai Ram' marks on the sides, and held my right hand to gently put it on the third finger. It was an exact fit, and it was precisely what I wanted from Baba.

NO CONTACT WITH FAKE BOY

Q: Thank You, Baba, You have answered the question beautifully. Now to Narasimhaiah's unanswered point regarding the bogus Sai Krishna of Pandavapura exposed by his Committee as a fraud and a cheat, he alleges that the boy had Your patronage.

Baba: I can assure you there is absolutely no connection between him and Myself. His people have several times attempted to arrange a meeting between us, but we have refused their requests. Of course, thousands of people, as you saw this morning, come here for darshan. There are others also who masquerade as My disciples or make money using My name. As this happens not

33

only here, but in other states and even abroad, we cannot do anything about it. They expose themselves sooner or later, as did this boy. I have absolutely no connection or relationship with such people.

Q: The Narasimhaiah Committee wanted to investigate Your miracles scientifically 'under controlled conditions,' as they put it. You rejected the proposal. Would You like to comment on this controversy?

Baba: How can science which is bound down to a physical and materialist outlook investigate transcendental phenomena beyond its scope, reach or comprehend? This is a fallacy on the face of it. One belongs to the MATERIAL and the other to a SPIRITUAL plane. Science must confine its enquiry only to things belonging to the human senses, while spiritualism transcends the senses. If you want to understand the nature of spiritual power, you can do so only through the path of spirituality and not science. What science has been able to unravel is merely a fraction of the Cosmic phenomena; it tends, however, to exaggerate its contribution.

GLOW-WORM IN SUNLIGHT

Q: That is true, Swamiji, but science is developing all the time, so that the metaphysics of yesterday becomes the physics of today.

Baba: Quite right, but it is still blind to the vast and invisible world of consciousness. The very fact that science is changing all the time proves its incapacity to investigate the ultimate and absolute Truth. Some time ago, scientists maintained that the atom cannot be broken, but recently they succeeded in breaking it. They are still ignorant about the realities of the pranic force behind the atom and the least of its components.

Science is a mere glow-worm in the light and splendour of the Sun. It is true that it can research, discover and gather a lot of information about Nature and its material functions, and use it for the development of worldly things. Spiritualism, on the other hand, reigns over the Cosmic field where science has no place. That is why some discoveries of science are useful while others can be disastrous.

As I have said before, Dr. Narasimhaiah and his group are like the Telegu men who go to the cinema to see a Tamil film. They will see only the dancing, the fighting and violence, the heroes and villains, the star with a beautiful face and these kind of superficial things, but they will lose the subtler aspects such as the music and the poetry, the plot, the dialogue, the jokes and the like.

However, as I have said again and again, those who want to understand Me are welcome here. It is the spirit of the investigation that is important. Foreign parapsychologists have come here and examined Me in such a positive and constructive spirit. You have seen their reports. They do not write letters or make public demands.

Narasimhaiah's approach was improper; that is why I rejected it. If it were not so, he would have been welcome. I do not call people here, so that they may bow to a God. I want them to come, see, hear, study, observe, experience and realise Baba. Then only, they will understand Me and appreciate the Avatar.

Q: Dr. Narasimhaiah maintains that according to science, "nothing can be created out of nothing". You have evidently negated this law of science with a transcendental formula for controlling Cosmic energy and producing paranormal power. Can you explain the mystery?

Baba: The formula that nothing can be created out of nothing is appropriate to the limited field and dimensions of science. It does not at all apply to the transcendental field and dimensions of spirituality. In the later field, anything can be created by the

Supreme Will. All that exists can be made to disappear, and what does not exist can be made to appear.

Our history and tradition, scriptures as well as literature, are full of such incidents which they call miracles. The material laws and formula simply do not apply to Divinity. For Me, this is not a matter of any mystery or mystique. WHAT I WILL, HAPPENS; WHAT I ORDER, MATERIALISES.

GOD EXISTS IN EVERYBODY

Q: The Vice-Chancellor appears to ridicule Your statement that "there is God in us all." He asks, 'Is this not pure escapism? How can God be so unsure of Himself?' Your rejoinder, please?

Baba: His questions contradict the very basis of Indian philosophy as well as that of most religions. All our scriptures assert that God is present in everyone. According to Vivekananda, 'God is present in all.' The only thing that is manifest and common to the whole world, and in fact, governs and directs the entire Universe is Divinity. Nothing else really exists except Divinity.

Mine is no escapism, but the fundamental and eternal Truth. I say so not because I am unsure of My own Divinity. It is my confidence in its absolute and total authenticity that makes Me affirm this fact. It is the scientists who are so unsure of themselves that they indulge in escapist theories.

For example, they say that the Moon is lifeless. Simultaneously they maintain that all matter consists of moving atoms. Now isn't the moon also a conglomerate of the same moving atoms? Then how can it be lifeless? There is no matter which does not consist of atoms, electrons, neutrons and protons, which are all constantly moving. This energy, too, is God.

So also, there is no human being in whom there is no Divinity. To say that there is no God in man is like saying that there is no

36

atom in the Moon or any large lump of matter. The omnipresence of God has been described in our ancient texts as, 'Ano Raniyam Mahatoo Maniyam.' (God is a small particle in the smallest of particles and a large mass in the largest of masses). In this context, how can one say that God is not in man?

NO PREFERENCE FOR WEALTH & POWER

Q: Another pertinent issue raised by Your critics is that You show a preference for wealthy and powerful people as against the poor and the weak in the matter of Divine gifts, miracle cures and individual darshans. Is this true? If so, why?

Baba: This is wrong. I never see or make any distinction between the rich or the poor. I only look at them from the viewpoint of their devotion, their desires, the sacrifice they are willing to make and their troubles. You were here this morning and saw hundreds of people, a few rich, the majority poor. Did you find Me making any distinction? All those I brought with Me here to this room were poor and weak, sick or troubled. In my view, those who appear to the world as wealthy or powerful persons really bring to Me their troubled hearts and sick minds. I cure them by asking them to surrender material wealth and power to spiritual peace and grace.

BABA'S GREATEST MIRACLE

Q: One of Your disciples, Col. Dilip Singh, wrote to BLITZ from Ludhiana to say that the present controversy triggered off by the Narasimhaiah Committee is going to be acclaimed as the greatest miracle of Sathya Sai Baba because it will establish His name, fame and faith throughout the world. Does Baba agree?

Baba: In a way, this is true. The result is good. It has tested and proved the faith of My devotees. That apart, would Karanjia be here with Me today but for Dr. Narasimhaiah and his campaign? So it is all for the good.

37

THE GODWARD PATH

WHAT, FINALLY, IS THE SUM OF SATHYA SAI BABA'S MISSION? "God-realisation through self-realisation", He answered. In this series of interviews, Baba has shown the Godward path to the realisation of Sat-Chit-Ananda-that is, Existence, Knowledge and absolute Bliss.

According to Baba, this highest state of consciousness or enlightenment is possible for every man or woman to achieve once he or she is liberated from the ego-bondage of body and mind to realise the true Self - that is, Jivatma. Jivatma is the abode of the indwelling God in man. It is the embodied essence of Paramatma, the Cosmic Spirit.

The Avatar's mission, according to Baba, is to help mankind dissolve the barrier of the ego and the mind with it. This will enable the embodied Jivatma to merge and fuse with the universal Paramatma, "the mighty ocean of nectar Divine," as He describes it, to raise mankind to a race of Godmen and Godwomen. Thus, Baba seeks to resolve the universal problem of man's alienation from man, God and Nature with the Sai philosophy of pure spiritual Love.

ESCAPE FROM TERROR OF EXISTENCE

Ruth Nanda Anshen, publisher of the well known "RELIGIOUS PERSPECTIVES" books, notes this as the most serious crisis of our apocalyptic era. "The crisis of man's separation from man and of man's separation from God - the failure of love," and holds it responsible for "the darkness and cold, the frozen spiritual misery of recent times." She evokes the image of HOMO CUM DEO to call for "a new formula for man's collaboration with the creative process and the only one which is able to protect man from the terror of existence."

Sathya Sai Baba provides the desired formula: only evolution to a higher plane of consciousness can save man from this terror, this darkness and cold, this frozen spiritual misery. The formula arises from Baba's expertise in the science of consciousness and knowledge of the cosmic dimensions of the nature of reality. Scientists, of course, scoff at Baba's emphasis on spirituality. Yet, the noblest of them, like Dr. S. Bhagavantam and Dr. Y. J. Rao, authenticate the Latter's supremacy.

IF ROCK CAN TURN GOD...

Dr. Rao is a noted geologist who heads the Geology Department at Osmania University. He was witness to the transmutation of a rock into God. Baba picked up a rough piece of granite to ask Rao what it contained. The geologist mentioned some minerals. Baba insisted, "I don't mean those, but something deeper!" Rao answered, "Well molecules atoms, electrons, protons ......" Baba wasn't satisfied. "No, no, no go deeper still!" Rao professed his ignorance.

Then Baba took the rock from the geologist, blew on it, and gave it back to Rao. The geologist was flabbergasted for the rock had been transformed into a statue of Krishna playing the Divine flute. Baba admonished him, "You see, beyond your atoms and all, God was in the rock, and God is sweetness and joy. Break off Krishna's foot and taste it." Rao found no difficulty in breaking it off the granite statue and tasting the foot. It was candy with a sweetness all its own. No wonder Rao confessed to Baba's biographer, Howard Murphet, "Science gives but the first word; the last word is known only to the great spiritual scientists like Sai Baba."

.... THEN WHY NOT MAN?

If Baba can transform rock into God - and we have Dr. Rao's word for the miracle - then why not the human being already

39

charged with Divine energy? Apart from His own prodigious spiritual image which encompasses millions of devotees, Baba uses the 3,000 and more Sai spiritual, educational and social service institutions throughout the country to spread His evangel with the object of transforming the common people into a race of enlightened Godmen.

However controversial some of Baba's claims may be, the integrated system of education and social service evolved by Him constitutes a model of its kind. It helps to understand and evolve man's total nature Here, the Sai philosophy with its five pillars of Truth, Righteousness, Peace, Love and Non-violence are not only being taught, but realised through the transmission of knowledge, skill, balance and vision to thousands of students and workers.

Thus, Baba plans to draw the whole community as well as the nation into His spiritual empire of love and cooperation. There is no expectation of any return for Himself. "Come to Me with empty hands," He says, "and I will fill them with My love and grace."

SELF-REALISATION IS GOD-REALISATION

This suffices to introduce the last installment of the interview to the reader. Let Baba continue to speak for Himself.

Q: From what Baba has hitherto said, it appears that Your mission is to enable mankind to rediscover and incarnate their lost Godliness. Am I right?

Baba: You are right. When man turns inwards to realise his true self, then God will become manifest to him. Self-realisation is God-realisation. In simple words, it is the realisation that you are not just a body and mind with the physical organs, but there is within you a Self - the Atma that is God - distinct from these perishable things. This Self is omnipotent, omnipresent, omniscient.

40

The comprehension of this truth puts you on the correct path to God-realisation.

So, I say to those who come to Me, 'You as body, mind and soul are maya, a mere transient illusion.' What you really are now and for ever is Existence, Knowledge and Bliss. You are the God of this Universe. It is you who are creating the whole Universe and drawing it in. You have the capacity to break the body-mind bondage and expand yourself to encompass the Earth, the Suns and the planets, the entire cosmos, within yourself. But to gain this infinite, universal individuality, you have to discard the miserable little ego-bound individuality, and create new dimensions, which cannot be found on Earth, and yet, must be experienced on Earth.

God is within you, seek Him, feel Him, embrace Him. He is there deep inside you, the Self. What matters is not the body, nor the mind, nor the brain. It is not the desire of the desiring, nor is it the object of desire, that matters. Above them all are YOU, the SELF, ATMA, GOD. All these are simply outer manifestations of the indwelling God. It is you who appear as the smiling flower or the twinkling star. You have everything within you. Find it. Discover it. Know it. Realise it. Then you will see that the world has nothing to offer which you can desire.

LIKE AN ELECTRIC CURRENT

Q: Still we have to live and function in the material world of body and mind. Does Baba suggest that we shed the corporeal frame to achieve realisation? That would mean death!

Baba: One does not have to shed the body and mind. They are like that fan and the electric bulb you can see above or the tape recorder you have brought with you. We have to use them. At the same time, we cannot forget the fact of the electric current which makes the objects worthy of use. Without the electricity they would mean nothing. So also, the body and mind are there, and you cannot destroy them, but you must realise that they, too, would be a corpse without the Divine Principle which runs through every body, mind and organ. Consciousness of this Divinity helps you to overcome the body-mind ego and rise beyond it to Self and God-realisation.

ATMA AS SOCIAL INTEGER

Q: If I understand You correctly, the way to enlightenment is to overcome the body-mind frontiers so that Jivatma, the embodied Spirit, can merge with Paramatma, the Cosmic Spirit. The fusion is God-realisation?

Baba: You have got it right. This is the function of the individual as well as of society. Every member must be enabled to realise this Atmic truth which embraces and integrates the whole world. It is not castes, classes, groups, families and communities which bind humanity together, but the fact that all mankind belongs to one and the same Atma that is God.

This single factor puts 'mankind' back into man to make him a socially conscious human being. As the Sastras say, Vasudhaika Kutumbakam, 'The whole world is one family.' This unity which derives from God can be experienced by everyone through recognition of the supremacy of the common denominator of the Self or Atma in every single individual.

TERROR OF NUCLEAR WAR

Q: So your objective can be summed up as a Brotherhood of Humanity to be achieved through the Doctrine of Love?

Baba: Yes, what else can save the world from thermonuclear fires? Everything points to the terror of that conflagration coming; and My mission is to preempt the fires by reestablishing Dharma and the spiritual Law of one God, one Religion, one Language embracing one Humanity.

I preach only one religion of Love for all, which alone can integrate the human race into a brotherhood of man under the fatherhood of God. I know only One Language of the Heart beyond the mind or intellect which relates man to man and mankind to God, thereby creating mutual peace and harmony. On this basis, I want to build One Humanity without any religious, caste or other barriers in the Universal Empire of Love which could enable My devotees to feel the whole world as their own family.

Q: Well said Baba, but wouldn't this dharma with its Hindu orientation conflict with the established religions?

Baba: No, it will not do anything of the kind because My objective is the establishment of Sanathana Dharma which believes in one God as propitiated by the founders of all religions. So none has to give up his religion or deity, but through them worship the one God in all. I have come not to disturb or destroy, but to confirm and vindicate everyone in his own faith.

DHARMIC WAY TO PEACE

Q: But how will that prevent a nuclear holocaust?

Baba: By removing all causes, sources, barriers and provocations of class, caste, creed, colour and race, and replacing the existing hate and violence with love and non-violence, I expect to provide humanity with an evangel of peaceful cooperation to replace the present escalation of death by destruction.

Karanjia: Thank you, Swamiji. I am all the more grateful to You because I really did not expect You to answer the whole long list of my questions.

THE SPIRITUAL REVOLUTION IS ON

(This exclusive article, written by Sri Sathya Sai Baba, was published in the October 9, 1976 issue of the BLITZ).

Millions of years of upward struggle have produced the present human society; thousands of seers and sages in all lands have taught man to see the Truth that underlies the panorama of Creation, to adore the Creator and to practice the virtues of humility, equanimity and service so that the spark of God that is enshrined in his heart might reveal its full Glory. However man has brought human society to the verge of total destruction. He has used his intelligence to pollute the land he lives on, the air he breathes, and the water that is the very source of his life. He has turned the mind which is the instrument of his liberation into a chain that keeps him in bondage. He has used Methods of Education, Codes of Law, Systems of Politics, Modes of Commerce and the Result of Science to imprison himself in prejudices, creeds and nationalities. The World is becoming smaller and smaller with every increase in the speed of communication, but neighbourly Love is not evident anywhere. Man truly lives when he feels One with All.

A revolution more powerful and pervasive than any that man has undergone so far, neither political, economic, scientific nor technological, but deep and more basic, is now on. It is the Spiritual Revolution. It sharpens the inner vision of man so that he can see his Atmic Reality. Its impact will surely envelop and enrich all human communities and transform mankind into a stream of Sadhaks flowing smoothly to the limitless sea of Divinity. India was for centuries teaching the World the ideals of Unity, Peace and Tolerance, and once again, She has to take the lead in this Spiritual Revolution. The Revolution has Love as both the means and the end. It will awaken the springs of Love all over the world in the fields of Education, Morality, Law, Politics, Commerce and Science. It will inspire man to living Service, revealing the Brotherhood of Man and the Fatherhood of God.

Everyone, wherever he lives, whatever his status, and whichever his faith can share in this Revolution, and be an instrument for the liberation of mankind from its own ignorance. The task of everyone is to do the Duty that has come upon him with a full sense of responsibility to the utmost of his capacity. There should be complete co-ordination between what one feels, says and does. Work is the best form of Worship. I am always declaring that My life is My message, for I take delight in spending all My time in acts of service fostering Love and Self-confidence.

I am exhorting the youth of the country to participate eagerly in various acts of service to the poor and the disabled. In the colleges I have established, I insist that the students should progress not merely in academic scholarship, but more in social service and in developing skills which will make them useful to the community.

Hard work and selfless service - these two alone can make our country united, strong and prosperous. I call upon everyone to fill the world with joy. Service to the human community is the best offering you can make to the Sovereign Lord.

BABA'S MESSAGE

All the religions demand that their followers be good, see good and do good. No religion approves untruth and injustice. Thus in essence, they are all one and have a common goal while in detail they may differ and follow alternative paths to reach the common goal.

God is one and only one without an equal, but known to different people in diverse forms and names. Form and name are transient and change with time. The unchanging truth, beauty and love continue to hold the devotion of the followers of all religions.

See this Unity in all living creatures. Serve them with love and selflessness. Banish your ego and pride, and realise God's Omnipresence. In the present environment, man is filled with jealousy and ego. These are the worst enemies of man. Only when he can get rid of them, will he be able to live like a man and have the ability to do selfless service. Service to man is service to God, and it is the noblest form of worship of God.

(BLITZ , October 9, 1976)

APPENDICES

SAI BABA: THE INEXPLICABLE AND INSCRUTABLE

- Prof. S. Bhagavantam

(Former Director, Indian Institute of Science, Bangalore, and Scientific Adviser to the Ministry of Defence, New Delhi.)

Science has become an all-pervading discipline and a force of our times. It has created around itself a certain aura, mostly by the glamour which its offshoots have caused in the minds of men. The common man, who does not understand its intricacies and its limitations, has begun to replace his traditional faith in God with a trust in science, and to seek by every means the material comforts it has been able to provide. Thereby, he has gradually reached the stage where he has started worshipping science as an all-powerful panacea for the multitude of human ills. His mental makeup has thus undergone a big change. Much of what is currently described as the incompatibility of science and religion is the result of a great deal of such misunderstanding. A law of science is often no more than a statement enunciated by some great individual intended to encompass the relationship between a group of observed scientific facts.

SCIENCE VERSUS RELIGION

Thus a law of science is automatically, and by its very nature, limited in its applicability to the same portions of experience that gave rise to the so-called scientific facts themselves. It is unreasonable to expect a law of science thus formulated to cover, explain, or comprehend an experience outside the area of the original coverage.

Religious experience, largely based on concepts like intuitive perception, faith in Divine strength and metaphysical orientation of thought processes, is one such area. In such an experience there is only a small overlap, if any, with that which is relevant to experimental science, the latter largely relying on sensory perceptions.

NON-OVERLAPPING REALMS

The facts of science and the results of faith are two large non-overlapping realms of human activity and have been so from time immemorial, each having its own distinctive concepts, methodology, function, goal and sense of values. The tangible results that flow from faith in God are as real to the incumbent as are the facts of science to a scientist who understands them.

Science has undoubtedly contributed a great deal to the material good and physical welfare of mankind. It has sharpened man's intellect beyond all recognition. It has also brought with it some well known drawbacks which merit the oft repeated encomium to man's achievements through the words, "Modern man has evolved into a being of intelligent gain, but has remained a moral dwarf."

Any individual who has lived and worked long enough in the company of his fellow human beings of the world at large, as we see it at the present time, will not, I hope, fail to recognise the missing basic values in human behavior as being essentially ethical and moral. These are being described by Sathya Sai Baba under various names like Sathya, Dharma, Shanthi and Prema.

REASON HAS NO ANSWERS

It is in this context that I would like to ask the questions: Is an appraisal of Baba on scientific lines possible? Do we have the capacity and right to analyse the phenomenon of Baba with the help of all the knowledge we have, and all that has been said either by Him or about Him by others? Can we explain His actions and doings? How does He fit into the pattern of accepted Indian traditions and Indian Philosophy, or for the matter, of any tradition and any philosophy, if He does fit at all? How is He different from others, and what is there in Him, either animate or inanimate, material or spiritual, ordinary or extraordinary that makes people flock to Him for solace, and come out of His physical presence so completely transformed when they are fortunate enough to get a personal interview?

So far as the writer's experience goes, these are questions which can be easier raised by the ignorant ones than answered. I had often made an attempt to find some kind of answers, and came to the conclusion that whatever answers can be put together can only be imperfect and incomplete ones. That too being done by each seeker of truth on the basis of his own experience, and perhaps only to his or her own satisfaction.

There are, however, certain general features of this phenomenon of Baba which almost every one observes. As one of the devotees had put it, "Amongst the many miracles which are attributed to Him and which one generally witnesses, one must not lose sight of the greatest miracle of all! This is the miracle of His unending and selfless Prema - His Divine Love."

HIS GREATEST MIRACLE

Every person that goes to Him thinks that Baba loves him most and in a special manner. I have checked and counter-checked this feeling from many a devotee, and the answer is invariably indicative of something superhuman or Divine on the part of Baba. To shower Grace and Love on a few chosen persons is not uncommon, but to let them flow equally everywhere, on everyone, and at all times is an attribute only of Divinity. It is something beyond human capacity.

Like all great teachers, Baba speaks in parables and appeals to the simple folk by telling apt stories. On many occasions, the most abstruse ideas are put across to His audience in such simple language that the more learned amongst His listeners feel quite embarrassed at their own inability to communicate even a fraction of their knowledge to those with whom they come in contact. Alas! What is the use of such learning, and who is to benefit by it?

GRACE FROM LOVE & SERVICE

He often exhorts His devotees to love God, serve Man and earn the Lord's Grace. He warns that life is short and is liable to be cut even shorter any moment and without notice. So while you can, you must dedicate your heart to Him who gave it to you.

Much of the Bhagavad Gita does not speak of this or that form of religion but, only speaks of the desire to find God and understand Him through disciplining one's own conduct. Baba does not prescribe or extol any one form of religion, but only speaks of the cardinal principles - Sathya, Dharma, Shanthi, Prema and Ahimsa - that should guide one's conduct in one's life and in one's search for God.

It is an oft repeated statement of His that the goal is one although the paths may be different and are many. The main plank of His mission amongst the people is to set them on the right path, the path of Dharma, or the Dharma Marga.

In this context, it is appropriate to recall that in the Gita, Krishna discloses Himself as an Avatar with the avowed purpose of His incarnation being not simply to uphold the world, but also to re-establish Dharma when it is on the decline, and help human beings to become perfect in their nature and within the limits of their capacities.

AVATAR OF OUR AGE

Thus, it appears that the essence of the Gita, recognized for centuries as the perennial source of much philosophical and religious thought in this country, and believed to have been originally conveyed by Krishna to Arjuna on the battlefield, is also the essence of what Sathya Sai Baba has been preaching and conveying to the many persons who flock around Him. Large numbers of them do so in the belief that He is the Avatar of our age.

The questions I asked in the foregoing paragraphs thus move over from the realm of common logic and rationale to the complex area of the evolution of mankind's faith through the vast ages during which, according to Indian beliefs and traditions, the Avatars of God have appeared amongst us from time to time.

The capacity to expound the Gita in a most appealing manner, the extolling and practising of moral standards to an uncommon degree, and the power to perform miracles to an extent are features that are known to have been, and will always be, shared by many great and evolved souls. Historically accepted Avatars like Krishna and Rama are believed to have done several things which we now call miracles besides preaching and practising the path of Dharma.

POWER WITHOUT LIMITATION

The fact that man generally tries to analyze highly evolved souls using methods alien to such areas of human activity, stands in the way of distinguishing one from the other. Thus endless discussions can and have always taken place in regard to what an Avatar is and how do we set about recognizing one, if it appears amongst us. This is not an easy task, and in fact, known methods of unraveling the secrets of Nature as commonly practised by us today are very ill-suited for the performance of such a task.

However, suffice it to state here that in the case of ordinary human beings, all powers including those that appear superhuman are acquired by some kind of Sadhana, and like all things acquired in one's life, they have limitations. On the contrary, in the case of an Avatar, all powers including those that appear Divine have been born as inherent features, and like all things thus born with one's life, they have no limitations.

DIVINE GRACE, NO MAGIC TRICK

India had, and still has, a whole gamut of miracle men and Godmen, ranging from charlatans and sleight-of-hand magicians, running through yogis and Siddha-purushas, and rising to Avatars and incarnations of God. It needs some effort on the part of any individual to separate the wheat from the chaff. Even as a blind person who has only tasted gutter water can mistake the water from a clear flowing river due to his inexperience, so also can an ignorant person easily mistake a magician's trickery for a Divine manifestation because of his ignorance.

Divinity and faith in God are not ready made dishes that one can demand, pay for and purchase in a shop, nor are they the products of modern science where one can mix together a few chemicals and cook them up in a laboratory. A great deal of effort is needed on the part of every individual before he can come under the protective grace of God.

Omnipotence should not be mistaken for a capricious exercise of power or an arbitrary conferment of favours on individuals selected at random who demand to be so selected on the basis of self-generated false standards. Divine grace cannot be pulled out by a penny in a slot machine installed by a municipality in the market place.

AN INEXPLICABLE WONDER

It is good to restate here that Sathya Sai Baba never had any schooling worth naming, and yet gives a masterly exposition even when He is on an abstruse philosophical concept. He never practices meditation or Sadhana to any extent worth mentioning, and yet performs miracles of the most inexplicable kind in quick

53

succession when He wishes to do so. He never has the need to work to keep Himself well, but always works with such perfection and zeal so continuously without exhaustion so as to urge His devotees to realise that work is the highest from of worship. Above all, He has never learned the details of life's complexities either in science, education or politics in the traditional manner, and yet instantly recognizes the point that may be troubling anyone in His presence and gives a forthright comment. That all these features appear so natural to Him cannot be dismissed as just being extraordinary. It is an inexplicable wonder, and is outside the realm of rational analysis.

I wish to conclude by repeating what I have said many times before on earlier occasions. I find it safer and more correct when I describe with humility what Baba does and what we see Him do, than when I analyze those facts to make an assessment of Him in terms of language, values and reasoning that we have evolved and learned while going through our normal experience in this world.

(BLITZ, September 4, 1976)

SAI BABA UNDER INVESTIGATION

- A. Roy

It was January 30, 1975 - my first visit to Puttaparthi - when Sai Baba picked me from the crowed for an interview. I was not at all prepared for this unexpected opportunity. As I waited anxiously on the right wing of the Mandir, I could easily recognize two parapsychologists from New York (Elendur Haraldsson and Karlis Osis) sitting close to me who had become a familiar sight at the Ashram due to their unusual activities. Unlike Dr. Narasimhaiah, who drew his hasty conclusions after sending a few letters by post, these two scientists of moral integrity had chosen a more sensible method of on-the-spot investigation to determine whether what was being published in the United States about Sai Baba was a hoax or whether there was truth in it.

Over a period of more than three months, they recorded statements of many men of unquestionable honesty who were expected to know Baba at a close distance and cross-examined hundreds of people from the crowd who had been granted interviews. Using movie cameras, they filmed many incidents of materialisation. In short, they had collected unimpeachable documentary evidence relating to the validity of the miraculous powers attributed to Sai Baba.

FACE-TO-FACE WITH BABA

I was sitting in the group of eight visitors who were asked to sit separately. Besides the two investigators, the group contained a couple from Los Angeles, a lady from Sri Lanka, a gentlemen from Hong Kong and a doctor from Bombay. Soon we were called into a small room, approximately 10' x 10'. We squatted on the floor facing Baba. He too sat on the floor instead of the chair behind

Him. Immediately on our arrival, as a gesture of welcome, Baba waved His right hand in the air, created some vibhuti (sacred ash), and distributed it to the group.

Calm and serene, Baba smilingly surveyed us with His fathomless eyes. I had the chance to watch Him intently from a distance of four feet. He looked exceedingly youthful and handsome. He was buoyant, cheerful and as simple in His expressions as a child which is a marked contrast to His normal reserved and imposing appearance observed in a crowd. Soft and sweet words effortlessly rolled off His tongue. Touched by His hospitality, we felt completely at ease. For a moment, I forgot that I was face-to-face with the most powerful and unique phenomenon of our times who is revered by millions in India and abroad.

Then to my great surprise, without any prior knowledge about me and my Hindi-speaking capabilities, He asked me to get up and sit beside Him to interpret His Hindi into English, which I did to the best of my ability. As I sat almost touching Baba, he leaned affectionately on My left shoulder, repeatedly placing His Right hand and arm over me in such a way that I could have detected even a small pin hidden in His sleeve if there was one.

AMERICAN COUPLE'S VEDIC MARRIAGE

Baba then turned towards the American couple (Mr. and Mrs. Krystal) and asked if it was their 33rd wedding anniversary on that day. Surprised, they replied in the affirmative.

"I will perform your spiritual marriage according to the Vedic rites," He said. Expecting something miraculous to happen, we all became very alert. Baba waved His hand in the air and materialised a golden ring with His bust embossed on it. He asked the lady to present it to her husband.

He next directed the couple to move further away, and put Himself in clear view of everyone, so that they could watch Him. He pulled His sleeves up and offered His outstretched empty hands to the group for a close examination. This time, as if not to strain our eyes, He did not wave His hand in the air. With His palm facing up, He slowly closed His left fist for everyone to clearly observe. There was absolute silence. As I sat abreast, I could see something glittering inside His fist. Using His right hand, He slowly pulled out a large dazzling necklace ('Mangal Sutra') about 30" in length and too big to be accommodated in a closed fist.

We became speechless at watching the incredible happen in front of our eyes. He explained the significance of the 40 rare gems (including diamonds) used in the necklace, which contained a large golden lotus with a bust of Baba on it. He handed it over to the husband, and asked him to put it around his wife's neck.

Looking towards the dumbfounded investigating team, Baba humorously questioned, "Tell Me, how did this happen?" There was no reply. " I am giving you repeated chances to observe Me closely and listen to Me because I know you are good at heart and are interested in helping humanity by your investigations," Baba added. For the following hour, many probing and interesting questions were asked, some of which are reproduced here.

MENTAL POWER THAT CREATES

Q: How do you materialise objects?

Baba: I materialise objects by My Sankalpa; it is a mental power that creates. If you develop your mental powers and purify your heart, you can also do it provided you love the entire creation as I do.

Q: What is the scientific explanation? Will science fully understand it when it has sufficiently developed.

Baba: Material science can never understand it. The scope of science is limited because it does not go beyond the manifest world. Science deals with experiments, whereas spirituality deals with experience and inner vision. I can see matter where the best microscope can find none.

Even the best doctor needs the help of an X-Ray film and the results of clinical tests of blood, urine and stool to diagnose a complicated disease. But I need none. I can give you the correct diagnosis straight away.

THE MIRACLES OF BABA

Q: Howard Murphet reveals in his book that you saved a man who was drowning in a well. How did you perform this miracle?

Baba: There is only one God, and He is omnipresent. It is the same Sai in all of you, and He is everywhere. When I saved the man from drowning, I did not move away from here. I was already there by virtue of My omnipresence.

Once an American was sitting along with Indira Devi of New Mexico where you are sitting now. As he sat here talking to me, his wife in America met with a serious accident while driving a car. I saved her immediately, and gave her the necessary assistance. I informed the gentleman about the incident, and told him that there was no need to worry. This accident was soon confirmed by her to be true.

DEAD BROUGHT BACK TO LIFE

Q: Why do you grant grace only to particular persons? How did you bring one Cowan from America and one Radhakrishna from India back to life when they were dead?

Baba: I consider certain points while granting grace to an individual. I grant grace when the devotee has fully surrendered to me and the situation is such that he would be greatly benefited or facilitated.

I brought Cowan back to life after his repeated heart failures because Mrs. Cowan would otherwise had to carry a dead body back home. Besides, this would help to spread My message among the American people for their benefit. In the case of Radhakrishna, I extended his life by 10 days only to enable him to write his will and complete his pending business and legal obligations.

Q: How do you know the past?

Baba: I also know about the future. I am beyond time and space. Nothing can impose any limitations on me.

Q: Can you grant grace to a country as a whole?

Baba: Yes, I can grant special grace to any country as a whole, if I so desire. I have granted you special grace by giving you repeated interviews, so that you may observe Me closely.

Q: How have John Hislop and some others seen a halo around Your head and emission of rays from it?

Baba: Thousands have seen it. Those who possess a developed mind and have love for Me can see it.

IN TWO BODIES AT SAME TIME

Q: As reported by some writers, how can you be seen in two bodies at the same time?

Baba: There is no limitation for me. I can be in thousands of bodies at the same time. Once a devotee prayed for assistance while in danger during the Chinese War. I left this body at the top of the roof, and went to help him. In the meantime, this physical body fell down and dropped dead. Cables were sent to Bangalore and other places, informing friends that I had died. Sandalwood was brought and arrangements were made for My funeral rites. Devotees gathered around My body and cried bitterly. At this point, I came back into this body, and told them that I was still alive and that I had left My body only to help a devotee in distress.

Q: How many hours do you sleep at night?

Baba: I do not sleep at all, but keep on thinking all the time. I switch off My bedroom light so as not to disturb anyone outside. I go to the bathroom and read letters from devotees and write something.

Q: When will you give us the next chance for an interview?

Baba: I give first chance to the needy and the poor. Today a lot of villagers had journeyed here from a distant place, and had no meal before coming here. I gave them the first chance because they had no money to stay here. I will call you when I am free.

AUTHENTIC PROOF OF DIVINITY

When the group interview was drawing to a close, one of the members of the investigating team (Karlis Osis) observed that an oval stone (1/4" x 1/2"), fitted on the ring worn by him which had earlier been materialised by Baba, was missing after he had entered the room. As some of us started searching for the missing stone, Baba took us one by one for a personal interview into an adjoining room. Unable to trace the stone, we looked towards Baba. He smiled, but made no comments. It was apparent that it was He who had dematerialised this stone.

After the interview was over, the gentleman asked for a magnifying glass and observed that the serration in which the stone was inserted in the ring was unaffected. After the inspection, he confided in me that if Baba could bring the same stone back on the ring, he would take it as conclusive proof of His Divinity. In a subsequent interview, to which I was again called to act as an interpreter, Baba blew air three times on the ring and rematerialised the same stone. The members of the investigating team literally shrieked with amazement. There was no more evidence required to prove the Divinity of Baba.

(BLITZ, August 14, 1976)

U.S. PARAPSYCHOLOGISTS' REPORT: NO EVIDENCE OF FRAUD

Dr. V. V. Akolkar of the Parapsychological Research Institute, Poona, has sent us (BLITZ) a copy of the official report made by Doctors Erlendur Haraldsson of Iceland University and Karlis Osis, Director of the American Society for Psychic Research. They came from the Chester F. Carlson Research Laboratory in the U.S.A. founded for the purpose of studying ESP and PSI phenomena. These experts investigated Sri Sathya Sai Baba's paranormal faculties at Puttaparthi. The report was presented by the scientists to the 1975 Convention of the Parapsychological Association at the University of California, U.S.A. Following, are relevant portions of the official report:

"During two visits to India, we met with Sathya Sai Baba several times. Our bid for formal experiments was rejected by Sai Baba with the comment that He would only use His paranormal powers for religious purposes. During our interviews He did, however, spontaneously display to us to number of phenomena..... At close range, we observed some 14 appearances and disappearances of objects, but none under controlled conditions. We will describe three.

"During an argument with Him about the value of experimentation, He turned the discussion to His favorite topic, the spiritual life, which in His view, should be as grown together with daily life as a `double rudraksha.' We did not understand the word... Sai Baba seemed to make several efforts to make its meaning clear until finally He gave up, and with some sign of impatience, closed His fist and waved His hand. He then opened His palm and showed us a `double rudraksha.' (Rudraksha is a hard berrylike nut usually grown in Nepal. It has several grooves or lines. A rudraksha with a double groove is rare and prized by sadhus).

"He took it back into His hand, and turning to Haraldsson, said He wanted to give him a present. He enclosed the rudraksha between both His hands, blew on it, and opened His hands toward Haraldsson. In His palm, we again saw a double rudraksha, but now it had a golden ornamented shield on each side of it, and a golden cross with a ruby affixed to it. We observed His hands very closely, and we could not see Him taking anything from His sleeves, or reach towards His bushy hair, clothes or any other hiding place.

MIRACLE OF THE RING

"Sai Baba presented Karlis Osis with a golden ring within which was embedded a large framed enamelled colored picture of Sai Baba... Once, when we were trying to persuade Him to participate in controlled experiments, He seemed to become impatient, and said to Osis, 'Look at your ring.' The stone had disappeared from it. The frame and the notches that should have held the stone were undamaged. When He made us aware of the stone's absence, we were sitting... several feet away from him. Since the stone could not be found, Sai Baba remarked, 'This was My experiment...'

"We were sitting on the ground. He stopped in front of a certain Professor Hasra, who was sitting to the left of Osis, and third to the left of Haraldsson. Sai Baba waved His right hand.. It was slightly above the level of our eyes. His palm was open and turned downward, and His fingers were stretched out as He waved His hand in a few quick small circles. As He did this, we observed a grey powder-like substance, called vibhuti, appearing close to His palm. It appeared just below and at His palm.

"At this stage, we obviously do not have sufficient scientific grounds for accepting claims of genuineness of the reported phenomena. It must also be stated that we were not able to detect evidence of fraud. He wears a long robe. It is buttoned from the neck down to about the bottom of the sternum bone. We had the opportunity of examining one of His discarded robes, and found no pockets or any other hiding places in it.

"We also had the same testimony from two research scientists and the wife of one of the two scientists who had a chance to examine a robe still in use. After each such production (ash and greasy substances), Sai Baba's hands were dirty, but neither we, nor the witnesses we interviewed, ever detected any such substance on His clothes."

(BLITZ August 21st, 1976)

GOD IS BORN AT PUTTAPARTHI

- A. Roy

"If someone asks you where is God, tell him that He is at Puttaparthi," so said Sai Baba to a visitor some time ago. Today, November 23, 1976, I am standing right on the spot where He was born exactly 50 years ago on November 23, 1926. Apart from a modern primary school, a Kalyan Mandapam, and a few white-coloured renovated temples, there is nothing striking about the place. People go about their business dreamily unconcerned and probably unaware of the historical importance of this tiny village. Lying like a mute orphan among the surrounding buildings, this vacant land on which Sai Baba left His footprints is heaped with tons of rubble and refuse carelessly thrown out by the neighbours, and there seems to be nothing godly about the place or the people around it.

SUPERHUMAN POWERS SINCE CHILDHOOD

"How did you know that Baba had superhuman powers even during His childhood," I asked His 86 year old uncle languishing under a thatched roof? "I used to dismiss all stories about His miraculous feats as mere rumours. One day I scornfully called Him to my side, and challenged Him to materialise two big lemons. He waved His hand in the air and immediately produced them from nowhere," replied the aging uncle.

There was not a single day in the village when a miracle did not occur. From empty bags, Sathya Narayana (childhood name of Sai Baba) would take out pencils, erasers, toys and sweets, and distribute them among His friends. Sitting on the sands of the Chithravathi River, He would create pictures and idols of deities, books, rosaries and crucifixes. From the top of a hill overlooking the river, He would show visions of Gods and Goddesses in their full splendour, and would pluck fruits like apples, mangoes, figs and grapes from a tamarind tree (now known as the Kalpa Vriksha) standing on the slope of the hill. When barely ten, He was an adept at music and dance, and at school He was unrivalled in the art of writing plays and poetry. The stories about this miraculous boy travelled by word of mouth far beyond the boundaries of this desolate valley, bringing thousands of enquiring visitors to this place.

BABA LEFT HOME TO COMPLETE HIS MISSION

At the age of 13, He threw away His school books and declared Himself as Sai Baba incarnated in response to the prayers of saints and sages. He left His home forever to complete His mission of restoring Truth, Righteousness, Peace, Love, and Non-violence, and to instill faith in God.

On October 20, 1940, Sai Baba gave the clarion call, "Oh ye, seekers of salvation, surrender to the feet of the Lord who has incarnated in human form. By His grace you will safely cross the impassable ocean of duality, birth and death." The chorus of this call still resounds through the valley and bhajan halls all over the world.

The rich and the poor, saints and sinners, all flocked to this place seeking solace, solitude and self-purification. As time passed, this place turned into a veritable crucible for mental and spiritual transformation where malificant and recalcitrant traits of mind are removed like dross, and the mind so purified shines bright in splendid colours of compassion and love.

WAVE OF SPIRITUAL RENAISSANCE

Every day a new page unfolds in the long, unending chapter on miracles. On June 5, 1976, a historic event occurred when Sai Baba materialised a silver-coloured metallic map of India, giving complete details for establishing important centres during the 46 years to come. He mentions the names, the locations and the nature of activity that will emanate from these establishments. Standing like lighthouses, these important centres are designed to illuminate the spiritual horizons of history for centuries to come. The map shows how Baba has Willed the future for posterity. Here is a being who has complete control over the forces which shape the destiny of man.

With their epicenter at Prasanthi Nilayam, mild tremors of a spiritual quake have already been felt over sixty countries in the world, and now a tidal wave of spiritual renaissance, unparalleled in history, is advancing to sweep over all the continents on the globe within less than 25 years as predicted by Sai Baba.

It is believed that there are now (1976) 20 million Sai devotees scattered all over the world. Thousands of them are writers, poets, journalists, doctors, engineers, saints, scientists and politicians of the highest calibre. To say that all these people have been bribed and brainwashed by Baba is utter nonsense.

VIBRATIONS OF LOVE AND DEVOTION

I do not deny the necessity of scientific investigations of this superhuman phenomenon, but as we go about it, we must not lose our sense of proportion and propriety. It is obvious from here that Sai Baba has become too big to be used as a guinea-pig in a scientific laboratory. It is ridiculous to suggest the use of an electron microscope to verify the existence of a phenomenon which is patent to the unaided eye.

Today is November 23, 1976 - Baba's 51st birthday. Sai Baba says, "Do not celebrate My birthday for I am never born. Celebrate the day when I am born in your heart." Today He will be born in the hearts of millions offering their felicitations on this great occasion. Prasanthi Nilayam has been decorated with paper

67

streamers, rangolies and floral tracks. A thin layer of cumulus clouds drift leisurely in the sky. The trees swing in soft murmur. There is something unusual about the place. The faces of devotees are beaming with a sense of jubilation. It is all smiles everywhere. The atmosphere is charged with the strong vibrations of love and devotion. One can really feel pure love rushing through his arteries and veins.

"MY POWERS ARE NOT ACQUIRED"

With an aura of spiritual glow radiating from His body, Baba appears on the stage. The anxious eyes brighten with the fire of longing within. The audience is excited and intoxicated with love. A heavenly bliss descends upon their beings. Up on the stage, visitors offer their floral tributes, and down on the floor, the devotees offer a garland of tears of joy and reverence.

Baba delivers His birthday discourse, "My powers are not acquired. They are Divine and beyond the comprehension of scientists. Science has limitations like a wooden ladder which cannot be used to reach the skies above. An Avatar comes armed with the four powers of Chamatkar (attraction), Sanskar (transformation), Paropakar (service to mankind) and Sakshatkar (God-realisation). He attracts people by His Divine qualities, transforms their character, exhorts them to serve mankind and grants them God-realisation. This is the purpose for which I have incarnated. Serve all. Love all. Especially those who accuse Me, for though misguided, they form part of the same Absolute."

Sai Baba sings :

> He who reveals Himself
> all over the cosmos,
> He who is ever near those
> who pray to Him,
> He who instills faith and

guards the faithful;
When He has come to
Puttaparthi,
How does it happen
You keep Him away from
your hearts?

For these 20 million devotees who keep Him close to their hearts and sing His glory today, believe it or not, God is born at Puttaparthi.

(BLITZ, December 11, 1976)

OUR PUBLICATIONS

FORTHCOMING PUBLICATIONS ...

OUR DISTRIBUTORS

Australia
Mr. James Somers
13 Hunter Street, Parramatta
NSW 2150
Phone : (02) 9687 2441
Fax : (02) 9687 2449

Canada
Sri Sathya Sai Books & Information Centre
290 Merton Street, Toranto
Ontario M 4S 1 A9
Phone : (416) 481 7242
Fax : (416) 498 0270 / 345 9212
E-mail : saibooks@idirect.ca

England
Sai Books UK Limited
21, Greystone Gardens
Harrow
Middlex, HA3 0EF
Phone : (181) 907 1267
Fax : (181) 909 3954
E-mail : saibooks@btinternet.com

India
Sai Towers Brindavan
23/1142, Vijayalakshmi Colony
Kadugodi, Bangalore 560 067
Phone : (080) 8451648
Fax: : (080) 8451649

Sai Towers
3/604 Main Road
Prasanthi Nilayam 515 134
Phone : (8555) 87270 / 87327
Fax : (8555) 87302
E-mail : saitower@vsnl.com
Web : www.saitowers.com

D. K. Publishers and Distributors P. Ltd.
1/4224, Ansari Road
Darya Ganj
New Delhi 110 002
Phone : (011) 327 8368 / 326 1465
Fax : (011) 326 4368
E-mail : dkpd@del3.vsnl.net.in

Europe (excluding England)
Sathya Sai Book Shop
Laurenzenvorstadt 87
CH 5000 AARAU
Switzerland
Tel / Fax: (62) 822 3722
E-mail : 113042. 2123@compuserve.com

Malaysia
Sathya Sai Baba Centre of Bangsar
24, Jalan Abdullah
off Jalan Bangsar
59000 Kuala Lumpur
Phone : (3) 254 5224 / 241 3646

New Zealand
Sathya Sai Publications
P.O. Box 56-347
Dominion Road
Auckland 1003
Phone : (9) 638 8210
Fax : (9) 638 8159
E-mail : ravi@titan.co.nz

Singapore
P. Ramanathan
Block 1M
Pine Grove No. 01- 43
Singapore 591201
Phone : 466 5983

West Indies
Ace Printery Fed Traders Ltd.
34-36, Pasea Main Road
Tunapuna, Trinidad & Tobago
Phone/Fax :
(868) 663 (2273) 663 2152, 3223
E-mail : ramdhan@carib-link.ne

U.S.A.
Jai Sai Ram
PO Box 900
Trinidad, CO 81082 U.S.A.
Phone : (719) 846 0846
Fax : (719) 846 0847
E-Mail : jaisairm @ ria.net
or
jaisairm @ rmi.net